The Uncertainty Principle

The Uncertainty Principle

Mark Kraushaar

WAYWISER

First published in 2011 by

THE WAYWISER PRESS

Bench House, 82 London Road, Chipping Norton, Oxon OX7 5FN, UK
P.O. Box 6205, Baltimore, MD 21206, USA
http://waywiser-press.com

Editor-in-Chief
Philip Hoy

Senior American Editor
Joseph Harrison

Associate Editors
Eric McHenry   Clive Watkins   Greg Williamson

A CIP catalogue record for this book is available from the British Library

ISBN 978-1-904130-50-5

Printed and bound by
T.J. International Ltd., Padstow, Cornwall, PL28 8RW

for my mother, Maggie Kraushaar

Acknowledgements

Acknowledgement is made to the following publications in which some of the poems in this book first appeared, sometimes in slightly different versions:

Alaska Review
Hat

Barrow Street
Chiropractor Claims to Travel Through Time

Beloit Poetry Journal
Chesterfield Kings

Chiron Review
Lester and Helen, The Personals, Alan

Gettysburg Review
The Uncertainty Principle, What It's Like

Hayden's Ferry Review
Everyone I Knew Before 9/11 Thinks I'm Dead

Hudson Review
Memorial, Chris St. George

Hopkins Review
Blind Date

Margie
Meeting Darlene, Traveling Through the Dark

Michigan Quarterly Review
Super Glide, Visit Wyoming, The Fallout Shelter Handbook,
Stop Me If You've Heard This, Begin Here

Acknowledgements

Missouri Review
Recent Cosmological Observations, Easy Money,
What the Dead Know, Stranger, Baffled

New Ohio Review
Third Street Muscles and Fitness, Cake, La Vie Ordinaire,
Maritime, Home Movie

Ploughshares
Non, je ne regrette rien: Edith Piaf in Concert,
The Cat and the Fiddle, Arthur

Thanks to Richard Merelman, Mark Kliewer, Richard Roe, and
Charles Cantrell.

Thanks to Andy Kraushaar for his help both with this book and the
last.

Thanks to Clive Watkins and Philip Hoy at Waywiser, Clive for his
considerable copy-editing skills, which were invaluable, Phil for
his close attention to every aspect of the book, front to back.

Thanks to Sara Obmascher at Leader Printing in Lake Mills for her
patience and good ideas and great good will.

Special thanks to the Wisconsin Arts Board for their support during
the writing of this book.

Contents

Contents

Foreword by James Fenton

First encountered as an anonymous manuscript in the finalists' pile, the poems collected here struck me as outstanding, first of all, for their sense of inner form, then for their careful and telling use of vernacular speech, and overall for their touching depiction of common life. On the formal question first: those of us who grew up with Anthony Hecht's poems as favorites will always think of them as sustained essays in the grand stanzaic manner: you couldn't begin to compose in such a way without an abundance of ambition and formal skill. But no one told me, when I was invited to judge this prize in Hecht's memory, that the strengths of the winner should resemble those of the late poet. Indeed, the prize would soon become a deadly award if that were the case.

There is form and form. In these lyrics, very few of which are longer than a single typed page, the shape of the poem tends to be determined by the forward push of the grammar (the opening poem illustrates this in a single sentence). The grammar itself is idiomatic, closely imitative of certain little quirks and tricks of common speech. The approach amounts to a sort of Low Style, appropriate enough for a subject-matter that includes the lives of workers in fast-food outlets, the visit of an overweight family to their local gym, and various touching recollections of marital breakdown.

I like the two gym poems especially, as studies of common experience. I like it that nothing is forced on to this material, or forcibly extruded from it. Photography has long been used to dwelling on such subjects – I think of Robert Frank's *The Americans* – and painting too. But poetry is often at risk of a certain sententiousness in tackling the "bone-weary, wounded world." Clearly our poet is not one for flash effects. I notice he prefers to end a poem on a muted note. But clearly too there is a sense of tender fellow-feeling, whether in contemplating the effortful lives of the gym-going acquaintances, or in quietly marveling at the contented lack of effort displayed by the obese family.

It is good to be, on the whole, well disposed towards your fellow man, but the children in "The Fallout Shelter Handbook" have a point when they test the limits of this benevolence, seeing the prospective shelter as a sort of Noah's Ark for pets and neighbors alike. Just what are the rules going to be? And is the mother, in this family, more alive to the problems of survival than the father with his reassurances? It's a problem. It could turn into an existential problem, like those worrying issues of relativity that appear so giddying and undermining to this disenchanted poet. It's a real pleasure – sometimes, to be sure, a melancholy pleasure – to make his acquaintance.

... and it seemed to me, as if I'd never known before, that this world isn't run like it ought to be run.

– from the screenplay by Horton Foote based on the short story "Tomorrow" by William Faulkner

Chris St. George

My best friend said once,
my best friend said in ninth-grade homeroom
to that rigidly grinning Mr. Sonny Sewell whose
flat-topped head seemed cemented to his
yard-wide shoulders, Coach – because
Mr. Sewell preferred to be "Coach"
in or out of class – Coach, my friend said
to this big-bottomed, thick-legged lug who'd clap
once before pulling down our world wall-map,
who'd clap once before speaking, who'd clap
once before sitting or standing or starting
study hall or football or civics,
Coach, my best friend said,
first wetting his lips,
then raising his hand and then standing
and leaning forward and knitting his brow,
Coach, he said to this Mister Sonny Sewell who swore
he'd slap any boy he ever caught crying in his locker room,
Coach, my friend said, this brilliant and lovely
and lonely kid whose mother drank Clorox
and died in her kitchen, Coach,
my friend said, who ten years later,
to find God, after trying everything else,
jumped in front of a semi in Richmond Virginia,
Coach, my friend said, who loved Scrabble,
and Brahms, Coach my friend said, first clearing his throat
and then raising his hand and suddenly standing, Coach,
he said, in football, in the game of football,
why is there so much pushing?

Cake

She's in the first booth left of the planters.
She's been waiting an hour now.
She's been waiting at the Watertown Family Buffet
with her little girl who's dreamed up
some kind of a costume:
giant glasses, backwards cap, taffeta gown
which is clearly for him, for Al who's
just now arriving, finally, and now

he's seen them, and now
he's walking over, and now
he's standing there, standing there,
husband and father, or boyfriend and father,
or boyfriend and father figure, except he's way too late,
he's too late times two and the party's over,
thank you, and, no, they're not having,
not the grin, not the story, not the hug.

The woman gets up, and then, face baggy with patience,
she nods to the girl, who scoots out too,
and they exit together.
So over the chips and spilt dip,
over the drained Pepsi and the big white cake
with "Al" in caps and quotes
he watches them go,
looks out at the parking lot,
opens his book.
Here's the waitress with her pad and pen.
And what in hell is he reading?

Meeting Darlene

It's first off how she's clutching
those groceries, but also it's how
we're standing four feet apart and not
facing quite squarely.
This is outside the Everett IGA
of a Wednesday in early April.
It's breezy and cool,
and she's just leaving
as I'm headed in.
Also it's how she's suddenly rushing –
Oh, she's got to get *going*! – so that added all up
when we say we'll stay in touch
we won't and we know it
and we know we know it which
takes place only after Hello and How
are you, which happens right
after the lamest wave and weird smile which
occur nearly seven years after our last day at Gehrke
Graphic Forms and seven years and a few odd months
after the after work party in which we could have,
and nearly did, head back to my place
three weeks after we first met
in the break room because
we were each of us eating an orange
and squirting juice all over a stack
of tax-rate database pages.
But here we are and, Hello and how *are* you,
how's Dan and where's Sara, and meantime I'm
thinking how I've really changed, not
only in a lot of little mental ways but, really,
science tells me by now all my atoms are
completely new and I'm
totally different.
Just saying.

Third Street Muscles and Fitness

It's rained all night,
and it's rained all day, and by evening
when I get to the gym it's started to thunder.
Still, here we are anyway, all of us, all the regulars,
George and Phil and Johnny B and Bob
and me and the big guy, the lifter from Janesville.
So first off George (who's zipping his coat)
asks Phil, who's on the treadmill and the only
one raising a sweat, will he run a mile
for every beer last night.
Which very funny, but Phil follows with, Hey,
I'm not drinking any more in '08
(beat, beat) but I'm not
drinking any less either, which, again,
very funny except we all know Phil has
problems with alcohol, but since he's getting no laughs
he looks up and on the tv over the rowing machine
there's the real life trial of a woman, blond
and twenty-three, a teacher who's
had sex with an eighth-grade boy.
Are you *kidding,* says George,
Are you *kidding,* says Phil, I'd clap her erasers,
and someone else, I'd polish her fruit,
and everybody's nodding yes and yes again
until, at last, George, who's had problems with school
and problems with money and women and work,
tells us he'd have majored in meredial reading
which is where the tv goes to an ad
and George waves once and steps into the weather.
So as the rainy wind flips his cheap rug straight
off his head like a flattened cat
it's strange, nobody's laughing, in fact, we're quiet finally,
Phil with his crashed marriage and the daughter
on drugs, and even handsome Bob
and Johnny B, even the big guy

with those silly disproportionate arms,
and for a moment, for a discrete, small portion
of what I will one day refer to as the past,
there's the five of us facing three
double-door-sized panes
of rattling glass:
rain on the awnings, rain over the windows,
rain over the gutters and rain
in soft, sparkling ropes along the curbs,
and into the drains and under the ground.

Fit Club Family Plan

If that fat bastard downs another Mountain Dew
he's floating home. And, so saying,
a vague smile rising like a blush,
the muscleman beside me toweled his quads.
But that was yesterday.
Today, at just past four, the same
fat man pads slowly through the side door
followed by his ample wife and acned, adolescent son –
past the treadmill, past the rowers, past the stepper,
past the trophy rack and free weights
to the snack machine and sits.
In fact, all three sit down
together on the vinyl mat
behind the water cooler, and while
the mother shares her modest bag of Cheetos
and a king-sized diet cola with the boy,
the dad begins a kind of push-up,
gives up and shuts his eyes and gently,
gently rests against the mother.
In a minute the boy,
this pink and softly wheezing, grinning teen, first
licking his fingers and placing the jumbo Coke
in easy reach, recounts his favorite tv show.
I don't know. I guess they're funny
in their way, the three of them.
Or, no, not funny but they're just
so pleased to be together here, not doing much
of anything, or, anyway, not working out
at least, but there's this easy,
intermittent laughter, a sort of mild,
unaccountable calm.

Maritime

My wife was nodding, Yes, sure, and, Yes,
and I was thinking of my parents, their sadness
and silence, their every evening's weeping,
whispery buzz beside the stove.
My wife was nodding, Yes,
and leaning forward when the pastor said, You're
like two ships passing in the night, and he seemed so
pleased I thought, So one's a brig-sloop, the other a tug?
Or one's a tanker, the other a trawler?
Troop ship and submarine?
Grain barge and gunboat?
I was quiet though.
It was August,
and there were two fans working,
and I thought of those salt-washed grey gulls
with their weird pink feet, and I thought of moonlight
shooting down the starways and cooling the decks.
I thought of two cruise ships next,
couples waving by the railings,
the faintest, farthest sounds of bands and laughter.
But there was nothing funny here.
He was talking or maybe she was, but
here we were, the two of us, our long, horizontal
journey almost over, no frenzied waves,
no reckless wind.
We were quiet, and she was crying,
or we both were, but we were perfectly still.

You Know What I'm Talking About

When you say this to yourself,
and when you say it softly again, once
as a question, once as a statement, and remember
some mid-summer evening with a few friends

in someone's backyard, when
you remember the one friend nodding that,
sure, yes, he sees what you mean, and when you think
of these friends and their low voices and someone's

quiet laughter at little or nothing at all
and remember the sudden sense
the evening was ending
and could never come again, that

inexplicable, tender mix of contentment and longing
when the urge to speak erased the path it traveled,
the moment, for a moment, perfectly still,
well, you know what I'm saying.

Stranger

I write poems for a stranger who will be born in
some distant country hundreds of years from now.
– Mary Oliver

Take that squat, bald boss slamming a file drawer shut
in central Aix of an early afternoon
in spring 3030.
This is for him.
But it's for a certain woman in western Quebec with
the leaking Bic pen in her right shirt pocket
who, though plain as a pigeon, will one
day become kind and wise beyond her years
for nearly no reason, though it is no less for the last
man to pass the fruit stand closest the First Bank
of San Juan the following May,
and equally for that man's best friend's son's
ex-girlfriend's mechanic's smiling mailman who will
have worn the same yellow visored
cap to his son's bar mitzvah as his father's
second wedding.
And, naturally it's for that happy bride but it's for anyone
living east of her cousin or north of her brother,
anyone who has ridden
the train to Peking and anyone
whose job it will one day be to teach animal husbandry
or bowling or brazing and likewise anyone
who will one day keep a cracked china bowl
by a leaking sink in his cottage near Zaire
as well as anyone who has ever once thought
or heard or mouthed the words, Federal Agent, freeze,
or, Carry your own damn bag or,
Leave out the beets.
But certainly, clearly, it is for all those for whom
this poem and all others will pass as unnoticed as a fingerling
trout beneath a sunken pier
in an imagined lake in central Maine.
And it is for anyone who will one day

stand at a similarly imagined water's similarly
imagined shore and think where in God's
name is God in this life,
what in the world has happened to the time?

Recent Cosmological Observations

One of the many implications of recent cosmological
observations is that the concept of parallel universes
is no mere metaphor. Space appears to be infinite in size.
– *Scientific American*

So, there's a sun like ours and a moon like ours
and a duplicate Earth with a town like this
and a street like this on a day like this
and there's a man exactly like me –
same wire glasses, same scratched thumb,
and dumb job, different shirt –
a man just like me who walks
past a Frank's Corner Deli, u-turns,
walks in and orders a corned beef
on rye, double the mustard, no mayonnaise.
Outside, an equivalent Checker Cab
pulls up and a similar lady in a backwards
cap gets out at a similar curb:
squashed Mars Bar, discarded sock, strutting pigeon
and all this under a wide, white sky with a glittering jet
and a crow below.
Of course, likewise, there's a smudged
glass counter and, in her crisp paper cap,
there's a girl whose tiny, terrible teeth also seem
tossed into her mouth like so many dice,
and just as I'm wishing this world's version
better, straighter teeth and love and long life too,
as I'm thinking how God on the Earth we know
seems absent or careless or cruel,
as an almost equivalent, nearly
identical God some place lolls dozing
in His giant cloud lounger, here, today,
three flies resettle on a split plastic spoon,
and as this Earth's girl scoops the last of the tuna
from a stainless tray she looks up and winks once
like we're perfectly grand.

Everyone I Knew Before 9/11 Thinks I'm Dead

postsecret.com March 13, 2005

I thought, Fuck work.
I was on the inbound 3 Train leaving Flatbush
and I thought, I'm getting off.
I thought, I'll walk around.
I thought, I'll get a drink,
and catch a matinee, and so I did,
or, anyway, I walked to Mickey's
read the papers, did the crossword and I was waiting
for my eggs up when all these sirens started,
then more sirens, but more and more
and so the waitress turned the tv on
and someone screamed
and everybody ran outside.
Everybody watched that black smoke belching
high across the river like they'd drilled a hole in Hell.
There was a kind of quiet though.

I stood there.
A little breeze began.
I thought, I have this one big chance.
I stood there on the corner, and I caught
a cab and got the Greyhound west that afternoon.
It's four years now, and I'm married and I'm happy.
Anyhow, I stood there on this corner
by an elm tree with its limbs
lopped off, and I remember by the curb
its branches sat in one enormous heap.
It was autumn.
A leaf broke loose and cart-wheeled through
a nearby yard in which a girl had made a foot-high
fence of twigs and fell asleep.
Clouds were passing and a car went by,
an ambulance, a car, another car.

La Vie Ordinaire

Monsieur LeBrun est une engineer chemiste:
on page eight of our ninth-grade
French 1 text Mr. Brown was just leaving for work
and behind him, always, always, there was Madame in her
pretty print dress and beside her the waving
twins Marcel and Marie –
Au revoir, Papa!
I'll guess the rest:
next he drives to Toulouse or Roubaix
and there's a big meeting on polymers, or pyrite,
heat flux, or octanes, and after his lunch,
he walks to the lab with his good pal François.
Think of one man pour a beaker of blue fluid
into a flask, while the other graphs
a special equation
or holds a test-tube in the light.
Later the two men sigh and say goodnight,
and Monsignor LeBrun climbs into his yellow Renault,
takes Rue des Gallois to Rue Saint Michel and arrives
back home where with six kisses given, six
received, the evening begins.
In fact, each evening starts with those same dozen kisses
for another decade at the end of which on a similar night
he opens his paper, sips his drink, eats, and sits
staring at a pink and avocado-colored plate
which like a little tv he can neither
focus on nor turn from.
C'est vrai, says Madame.
I guess we want to make sense, she says, except,
here's this whole improbable, bright scene before us,
and we're peevish and stuck, and then one day
you're rinsing a cup and it's like the heart
takes off for Bermuda and you rise right out of your shoes
and think how easy it is, how like a trick of the mind
to simply be happy, and as the Earth turns

into a map there comes a moment it feels
like forgiveness and thanks and when
you want to dive you dive – *c'est vrai!* –
and recover soaring upwards
by thinking it so.
I've met someone new, she says,
It's true.

You Have One New Message

Frank, hello, it's me, she'd said.
It's Sarah, she'd said.
She'd called about a book, plus
her blouse and so wondered could she come over.
Say, Monday, she'd said, or any day.
Goodbye, let me know, she'd said.
Let me know, she'd said.
There'd been a shyness though, a kind
of an urgency but the call wasn't new, it had been
two years and he wouldn't erase it.
It's almost August, nearly noon,
and next door, Mr. Ingalls, having washed his big Buick,
begins now to dry it with the first of a few soft,
indeterminate cloths: dries the windows
and windshield, then the doors,
then the bumper and trunk,
headlights and hood and with special
emphasis even the hubcaps, even the tires.
He dries the driveway with the leaf machine.
What was it Sarah called him?
Mr. Productivity.
Mr. Industrious.
Frank looks on a minute more,
then turns to the phone in its blinking black
cradle by the fridge.
He presses Play, and then Rewind,
and Skip, Skip, Skip. Then he listens.
Then he listens again.

Super Glide

When my friend said he'd had enough
of Janet's Friendly Grill he'd done eight months
as fill-in counter man and prep chef and he roared up
late one Friday night, pulled in and parked
between the dumpsters and the vent fan.
It was beautiful too, fringed seats, shorty
pipes, and custom bags, chromed heads,
chromed forks, chromed carbs,
plus monkey bars, but what was beautiful
was how this strange, soft man arrived

a moment after closing, waved and made a vee sign.
But it was how he'd revved the engine once,
removed his shades, and then
dismounted, slowly though, not
like his knees were shot, which, of course,
they were, but with a kind of sullen,
movie-world, deliberating cool.
It was as if this pudgy-fingered
flakey-bearded man, too shy to date,
who kept six cats had overnight become so

hip and happy that standing there
and grinning like that, grinning and grinning
as he stood there in these new black leather chaps
and studded jacket, he'd found out some huge secret secret.
It was how he'd timed it too, but it was how
in the light of the buzzing Pabst Blue Ribbon sign
we stood around him, three busboys and the fry cook,
all of us as lost as ever except that we
were grinning with him, smiling
for him, and for a moment, free.

Nothing Bothers Me

My mother never mentioned heaven.
Kooky talk she said.
I was six or seven when I'd lie in bed
completely freaked about it too, it death, I mean,
it death which she promised wouldn't happen
soon except that anytime was way too soon
and so she'd slowly reason back,
Well, no one *wants* to die, which
if not an answer wasn't any comfort either.
As far as God goes believers say
He's everywhere.
He's everywhere and everything, which,
fine, okay, except deep down we almost know
there's nothing's coming which is just what's wrong, so
we're a little jumpy except remember, and I hope this helps:
this is not the nothing there'd have been if there
were never anything. The nothing coming
is the one that's bumped and bordered
everything – friends,
trees and travel, little towns,
and cities, planets, love, and luck.

Rapunzel To Her Daughter

Your father loved my singing voice.
I loved his smile.
I dropped a braid and told him come.
He loved my feet and hands, he said, and then,
I mean, and then the feel of me.
Afterwards we watched our silver river stretch
beyond the village through the fields,
we'd make a life.
But prince?
Your dad sold feed grain out of Yorkshire.
There's no harm in that, no shame there, besides,
my gold-plate fabulist was in his cups, and when he said
he'd be back in a week I winked. I was glad
he thought enough of me to lie.
Years later I remember sitting in the yard
with you. It had rained, the roofs
were shining and the grass
was jeweled and when I'd close my eyes
I'd picture him beside the gate and place you in his arms.
Far away I heard a church bell,
and I thought about my tower room above the trees,
our shining river, my unmarried bed.
I thought of his uncertain searching through the world
and I thought about a joke he'd said and how
he'd smiled and pulled my shawl around me,
a little thing, but I remembered as he left
that day he waved, and turned
and waved, feckless, insufficient,
puppy of a man, no man, and I said
his name and I said come back,
but softly, softly though,
no one the wiser.

The Lone Ranger

Who was that masked man?
Well, it wasn't *me*, Nancy laughed,
shoving me once and running upstairs.
But wasn't it *unlikely*, that dashing masked
rider of the plains, the fiery horse with the speed
of light, the gold coins under the stump,
those dozen varmints by the Circle K.
Still, there could have been nothing
so unlikely as how on this strangest of days,
both parents away, her brat brother sick at her aunt's,
Nancy Jodzio-Flores, the prettiest girl
in twelfth grade called me up,
called *me* up to watch, she said, her dad's
new, color console tv on her new mother's
modern sofa. Come over, she'd said,
come over, come over, so I did,
on a repainted Schwinn with a rubbing
rear fender and three broken spokes.
Unlikely?
Unlikely was how, minutes after the show,
standing by her bureau in that little pink room,
trying to look natural, trying to seem normal, I was
thinking, I'll always remember this, which I would and do
because atop her flowery bed, arms out, she,
Nancy Jodzio-Flores, was entirely nude,
and for that moment, stepping
forward, I thought of a hearty Hi-Yo Silver,
and I thought of that grateful, waving sheriff
at the Big Dollar Saloon:
I could not *believe* my good fortune.

Alice Beatty

She could say only that it
wasn't working, her life, not really,
not quite, and that if it were wishing and worry
could lead her to heaven she'd be living large even now.
Cryptic and comfortless, she would say only
that it wasn't working.
And then, one morning, the strangest thing:
she couldn't go forward.
Her bus pulled over, and she was about to get on
when instead she just stood there.
Next day it happened again.
She'd meant to go to work, she'd wanted to,
and the bus came and she stood there and stood there.
The sun shone, a dozen geese
veed south, and the bus,
of course, the bus
coughed its deep cough and shoved off.
That night it happened at home, first rinsing a plate
and then brushing her hair – she wouldn't move.
She stood there.
She stood there and then, gazing at the tiny,
moon-shaped scar along her thumb as though
mounting a silent, secret fight underneath,
she slowly moved as she must.
Friends said snap out of it.
Her friends said, Alice, *please*.
And her husband, when he'd had enough,
and when she'd watched him fold his clothes and pack
and find his keys, even then she wouldn't say wait
and she couldn't explain and later,
that week when he called,
(How *are* you? he'd said)
even then, his voice pushing gently
through the phone, she regarded the desk, she looked
at the standing lamp and pictured it's five-foot cord

and three-pronged plug and socket
and secret passage of electrons.
He was talking,
and then he was still.
And then he was talking.

The School of Meditation

Each week there to greet us was our teacher
Mr. Hume, smile, smile, smiling, smiling, smiling like
isn't it ironical, like isn't this almost comical,
all of you thinking you're here which
you are but never in the sense
I mean which is here in the moment,
here as in perfectly centered in present time
which, no, I'm not either but clearly
I'm closer than you.
In fact, next thing Mr.Hume
would lead us down a long hall
to a yellow room with flowers and folding chairs
where he would explain that to be in present time we
would need to be *fully realized*, or "enlightened"
was another word, but enlightened
was this other world into which
we would be dreamily, dumbly
bumping forever unless we would now
sit, backs straight, feet on the floor, eyes closed,
and, with our hands on our laps like resting birds,
slowly say this secret word, but silently, silently,
only to ourselves.
And so we did, I did,
except always afterwards,
stepping into the street, then catching the bus,
then finding a seat, I looked and I looked and looked,
and there was the world with its places and days
and around it, peculiar and familiar, this single,
continuous moment, this gorgeous,
and impenetrable present.

South Bend Graphic Forms, Inc

Jimmy couldn't focus
so maybe his mind was on the great
enduring things, but he was nerdy
and a little dirty too
and he had a back-bent, grieving
diligence and lumbered through his meager life
as one who, were it not for his neck, would have left
his hay-filled noggin in a taxicab.

The ladies hated him.
He'd been in their bad books from the start
and couldn't tolerate his downward twisting drift
since when they could have helped him out and wouldn't:
they felt their own god-given goodness kept
imprisoned by convenience,
incapacity and anger.
Jimmy foundered.

And so it was amidst the cooing hubbub
of wedding jabber, shoe talk, and hissing,
spinning gossip they concocted a story
and made a call
and got him canned.
Tough when it suited them, leery-looking,
tender or teary as the occasion urged,
they bought him a shirt.

On his last night, though, walking to his car
Jimmy paused to find his keys when blond, low-
lidded Mary Ann placed her open hand
along his arm and wished him well,
and Jimmy, smiling and trying,
high-minded and harassed
under the crossing stars,
Jimmy turned and went his way.

Icarus

At first I felt bad because
I didn't feel worse.
But then I felt bad.
I should never have married,
she should never have left.
But it's everything.
I think it's mostly the quiet though
which is strange since that's what I needed
so much of.
It's my job, it's the town,
it's the neighbors' small dog.
It's the waiter's shaved face and stained shirt.
But it's everything, conspiring breeze,
crushed can, man with a cane.
Still, sometimes just walking along
I rise right off the pavement.
I never go too high: accounts of this
are all wrong – no wings, no wax,
I've never been over the ocean,
but over the traffic and over the trees.
I want to know how this works and remember
tomorrow: it's, I think it's a kind of intramural release,
I think it's secret, inside, letting go. I know
it's in the mind or even the heart but
in the morning, every morning,
there's the same inevitable silence,
the same invisible, zillion tiny cables and cogs
that link me to Earth.
I think it's just gravity, or I know it is,
but it's a little like sorrow: it must be, I feel it.

Flight 868 to Seattle

A man stands at the corner
pitching and swinging. Now and then
he jumps up for a line drive but it's mostly
this pitching he does, mostly this slow-motion swinging.
Raising his arms and watching another home run
arc deep into nowhere, he waves the wave
of the famous, winds up, pitches
and swings, then lopes
to the mailbox and back,
invisible bat, bright cap.
Make it late spring, early summer.
Behind the man there's a small store
with a blinking red X and drawn shades,
and I imagine other men likewise pretending
except for them it's that they need only open a magazine
for someone to love them – a woman bent one way
then another over a sink, a man strapped to a chair,
suit yourself. Now and then there's the ching-
ching of the register drawer as from under
the harsh light into the street a man
steps with a plain paper bag.
But it's midmorning of a Tuesday in June
and as I'm watching all this, as I'm waiting
for the airport shuttle at State Street and Main, I
imagine myself in two hours, five miles over the Earth
and pretending we're as safe as saints, pretending my best
thoughts can keep us aloft.
Wired and worried, pretending and praying
in our own invented blends, we're a rivet's width
wide of oblivion.

Now Playing

The buck private boarding a train says
after he's back he'll start a strawberry farm
or he might try steam pipe repair.
Well, big smile, all aboard.
Of course, we all know
he's shot dead or loses his legs, but it's here
the man in the next row whispers this tip:
If you want to hear God laugh
tell Him your plans.
So his wife nods yes, and says, Shsh, which
is precisely what my own wife used to do: she'd
nod yes, and, yes, yes, and say, Shsh.
Of course, she's the ex-wife now,
but as the train chugs out of the station headed for war
I picture myself and my future ex-wife meeting God
in His huge, quiet office with a lot of plants
and, sure, we're plenty jumpy but God
seems *very* nice *and* He is *really* listening
so I explain how we plan to marry and might
buy a house when suddenly God clears His throat
making the perfect point
at the right time exactly: Forget it.
Up front meanwhile there's lot's of bombing and bleeding,
but I think of this huge party for God and with all
the various saints and angels gathered around
He tells the story about my big plans
in music, and my two years
driving cab, and my six
months selling wigs, and my four years as a welder
and, okay, I have to laugh myself the way He says it.
There's one about my usual poor choice of mates,
and another about some places
I've lived and some friends I've made,
but by this time the credits are rolling and everybody's
filing out except for the couple in the next row

who sit there sobbing away because though
there's a happy ending except for the legs
the world seems so sad that even,
or even and especially, the best, most
beautiful stories make us start boohooing
like there's no tomorrow when even
if there isn't there is.

The Secret

Sometimes I tell people what to do.
Buy a cat, ride your bicycle,
read more fiction, take a nap.
But to the jumpy sad-sack
in seat-fallen trousers
and the dirty cardigan,
to heart-filled Melvin
with his greasy, flaky hair,

I say skip the nervous-laughter, would you?
I say this because beneath the laughter
there's embarrassment, and beneath
embarrassment confusion
and alarm, and underneath
all that the winds
of failure flying up his sleeve.
You'll be stooped and crooked one day

and you'll be derelict
and haunted just like all of us.
I say, Relax. The bone-weary, wounded world
is hard on everyone, it's life, just life,
and though such truth as it finds
reveals no more than more
of the same we jig along
unaccountably searching for clues.

Chiropractor Claims to Travel Through Time

– Associated Press

I was driving home after work
and it was a late afternoon and warm out
and breezy too, and in what painters call
the golden light a dozen cows stood
grazing on a hill.
I'd seen them before, and yet, I can't say –
pulling over I watched two more under a huge
spreading oak and beyond them a boarded barn
and a billboard hawking cement.
I closed my eyes
and I thought of myself
in this single moment moving in time,
and I thought of my patients and family and friends,
and placed them all in luckier days.
Where's the harm?
Couldn't it help?
I pictured Allen's slipped disc and Mary's
crimped neck, and I thought of Frank's bad back,
Brad's huge, hectoring sadness.
It was no more than that, except I remembered
my father on our screened porch reading the paper
and how looking up he'd turn a page and double it.
We do our best, he'd say, we make our own beds,
and then the sun might illumine a magazine,
or a little air stir a curtain.
He tried, I know,
but every evening
watching him watch the tv
I wondered what clues had eluded him.
Constricted, uncontent, incomplete,
what secret had he'd missed?
It was a late afternoon and warm outside
and in that still, soft light, I thought of them all,
and together with the sky and the field, a tractor
moving into the sun,

the curving indifference of the road itself,
the whole undefinable bubble
seemed perfectly possible.

Bike Routes of Jefferson County

Right after the tracks
where the Punzel farm begins
a few crows meet for seeds, and I slow down
and think of my father who packed a small, thumbed,
soft-bound bird-guide when ever he traveled.
At the corner I turn down County Q,
up Veith Road to Box Elder where, gathering speed
in a gentle descent, I imagine the great cyclists of history:
Hinault and Indurain, Merckx, Bartoli and, Antequil,
but today I think of Fausto Coppi himself,
Il Campionissimo: winner of La Flèche Wallone,
winner of the Giro de Lombardia and Paris-Roubaix
and seven-time world road-champ, and One Hour King:
Il Campionissimo, champion of champions.
It's early August.
I pass a cornfield six feet high,
the ubiquitous Bud Lite can and dud truck
and then somebody's glove.
On my left there's a yard with a Farmall Cub, a three-
railed fence, and a hill with low trees and a dozy Holstein,
and in the blue distance over my shoulder an exhausted
bright peloton ribbons slowly up Toppe Road,
past a ruined silo and a barn so old
you could poke a finger through.
Il Campionissimo.
I take Neuville past Kunz and over Cottage Grove
to Hope Lake Road where the herons are, those
feathery pencils, and now and then a hawk
coasts out of the trees or some
dust-colored, bright-billed bird sings, This,
sings, This is what I wanted, this,
and I think of my father again who loved
birds for being so alert, I think, though I'd never
have asked and he wouldn't have said.

Funny

My friend Alex liked to hunt
and he showed me how one winter
on his belly by the swings.
So because I'd bugged and begged them both together
and alone, because I'd earned the money on my own
and joined the rifle club or promised to,
my mother sighed and said alright,
and my father said okay and I
sent away and waited,
and in just three weeks my Sears single-shot,
bolt-action .22 arrived, and I took it apart
and oiled it on my bed.
I oiled it and aimed it, aimed it and aimed it until one
late afternoon while my mother was at work
I shot this rabbit in the yard behind the shed,
shot at him anyway, ran back and got
another bullet and this time killed
him dead, or pretty close,
his legs were twitching
and I brained him with a shovel, so when
this young woman up the block says she's vegetarian,
when she says she's seen enough of guns to last
ten lifetimes, I, who'd stood those awful
moments in our yard
as quiet as a painted post and looked down
all my angry, idiotic fourteen years
and finally smashed that
rifle on a rock and split the stock
and bent the barrel in a tree, I,
who should have been the first
to see exactly what she meant
and could have mentioned how this small
sad thing had changed me for the better, instead

turned smiling to her smirking husband: Vege*ta*rian,
he said elaborately, and shut one eye and with his finger
fired at the broad, blue sky.

The Personals

Car Crash 7/30 Thompson Dr.
I drove by and saw you lying there surrounded by onlookers.
I've said mantras for you – would like to hear you're well.
– Isthmus 8/30/7

I'm fine,
maybe that's what she thinks
and sits there by a window in the kitchen,
examines the page and folds it, doubles and drops it.
I'm fine, or, Mister, thanks.
A moon-appointed sky illumines the yard.
Of course, because she ought to be
grateful, she pictures her schools and jobs, her husband
and home, all those backwaters and bayous,
so that for a moment she *is* grateful,
sure, or she's trying, look:
she thinks of the farms and the fields,
she thinks of the forests, she thinks of the gentling
clouds and the wheeling birds and how under the same
blue bowl and bearing her own
secret search she's made do.
She thinks of a world wall-map and Liberty dime.
She thinks of a tin fork bent pretending
the mind can do anything, thinks
of talking to Alice, brushing the cat,
thinks, Give me a break, and, Why bother,
but she thinks of thinking of thinking, and then
a dog barks, somebody coughs, and she pictures
a blurry Monday, an unaccountable
Tuesday, an inevitable Thursday in which she'll be mowing
the lawn or changing her dress when will come this
sudden pressure, or maybe an ache
down one arm bringing back
some unearthly calm. She thinks,
It will be a moment before a moment
that will seem, in the pure clarity of its absence,
miraculous.

The Fallout Shelter Handbook

It might have had an eagle on it.
It was more a booklet than a book,
and the cover showed this family living underground.
Make it autumn 1962.
One night Dad said we'd share
a shelter with our next-door neighbors,
and then my brother said he found a snake
at recess not near the seesaw but beside the swings.
My father asked me would I like more beets,
so I said, No.
No *thank* you.

Next my sister asked him,
What about the Napolis?
Then my mother said there wasn't room.
But what if they would knock, for instance?
We would let them in, my father said.
And what would happen if the Stevensons ran out
of water? Well, we would let them in, he said.
Would we have to save the Johnson twins?
And what about the Stirlings?
Would we let them in?
We would, he said.
And what about my snake? my brother asked.
And what about my cat?
my sister said,
and what about the Blinskis,
what about the Craig's new hamster,
and Mrs. Musiel, and that kid, that one
who likes to fight?
Would we let the Faners in?
They could build three shelters.
We would let them in, he said.
We would let them in.

Begin Here

He'd simply asked if for once in her life
she couldn't be quiet.
So she said he'd never loved her
and he said how could he after what
she'd done, so she said he'd strung her along
and he said, well, he needed someone to ruin his life.
When they were calmer though,
when they'd gone about the business
of the afternoon, she walked over and stood
by his desk.
She said, The only good thing, I mean,
about you, I mean, is those stories you write.
And then she paused and walked out.
They'd spoken by phone – she wanted the cat
but that was months ago, so begin now with his glasses
and how he'd reached for them, knocking
his water off the night stand.
He'd been going to get up, he'd started to
except instead he lay back as though on a slow,
white river going nowhere.
Moments before this he'd heard
his neighbor talking softly to her daughter next door,
and just before that he'd closed his eyes and just
before that he'd heard her shouting to Please
keep your voice down,
and just before that he'd heard the girl's
voice shrilling into the trees outside the window:
a robin she'd seen, some ants
by the fence, a squirrel, the sky, the robin again.
On his side, his face at rest on his forearm,
he listened to the two of them, her voice
and then the girl's, mingled but suddenly

separate, slowing and stopping and starting again.
And then, watching the sun's small, unremarkable
pattern cross the opposite wall,
he reached over his shoulder.

Poetry Noir

See this?
Well, it's a .38 but I call it a piece.
I call it heat and I like to clean it in the kitchen
while I'm eating. I like to spin the cylinder,
and I like to pull the hammer back
and point it like this,
and like this and this.
Hey, you, hey Glamorous – Yeah,

you got ears – put a star in your crown
and pour me a drink.
Sure I like a little drink, what of it?
Just maybe I like slamming the glass
on the table: ahh.
Plus sometimes I like
to walk to the window, and part the curtains
with the barrel for a look around

because who knows there isn't
somebody out there, somebody parked
at the curb in a dark suit
and creased hat, for instance,
someone like you with a book in his lap,
someone trying to get at the meaning of things,
taking a note now and then, leaning over
and looking up, and leaning over again.

Stop Me If You've Heard This

In one week Duncan will marry
the woman he loves. Call her Doris.
There'll be a splashy dinner and a fancy dance
and everyone who's anyone will be there.
Now say the braless and still
more beautiful younger sister who's
constantly ogling him, constantly bumping
and brushing against him with her heavenly chest,
say one day this pretty sister invites him over,
to move her huge bureau and heavy stove.
So, okay, be right over, happy to help
and ten seconds after he's arrived she says
how about we make out this once.
She will never, never tell and that's a promise.
Plus she's fixed up her bedroom especially.
She makes him a drink.
Think it over she says.
He sits there.
He sits there a little more.
Then he flies out the door, over the lawn
and on the corner at the curb there's his whole
future family clapping and waving
because clearly Duncan has passed the test
and now he is one of them.
And the moral of the story?
Always leave a condom in the car which,
sure, very funny, but meantime in Braintree
or Akron the real Duncan stands at the curb.
There's Mom, there's Dad and Doris, and even
the little dog Whiskers, but right now something –
a snigger, a twitter –
something grabs his attention, and he glances
up and there's the wide, white cloud-elaborated sky
sweeping left.
How weirdly the world seems tipped in his favor.

Is it luck? Is it fair?
Is it good? Is it God?
He listens again.
It reminds him of thunder,
it's an almost sound he can nearly hear –
the whole world rumoring, whispering.
He thinks of it walking home.
He thinks of it mowing the lawn
and going to sleep,
a last laugh still clearing the trees.

Visit Wyoming

My father drove because he always drove.
My sister sat up front and so did my mother,
and behind them in the back seat,
I read Boy's Life: how
to read Morse Code and so on,
how to tie a half-hitch, how to pitch a tent.
There was always a picture of the good scout too,
kneeling by a fallen bird or a berry:
it was something about
the angle of his forearm at rest on one knee such
that plain common sense never looked so calm and combed.
My father though.
My father drove because he always drove,
and as he turned up Washington Ave,
we slowed to a stop at the lights,
and to the left, a few stories over the street,
a metal boat hung suspended from a huge, yellow crane.
My father said cables held it, cables
or ropes, he couldn't say, but
there'd been a road crew
at work on a bridge that day.
My mother turned to me and winked.
There's somebody fishing for crows she said,
and then, in a minute, as the light changed
my father lit a cigarette,
and I said, Quit it,
it's making me sick, and he said he wouldn't,
it wasn't, and I said something else, and he said
something back and we were shouting by now which
is how it always was – or so it seemed.
It's years ago but today, this afternoon,
as my father's nurse explains
he's had another small stroke.
His stiffened lungs are working like a saw.
Out his window past the trees a billboard shows

clear water, and mountains and a bank of white clouds.
Visit Wyoming, the sign says.
And in the corner, lower left, there's
a man, a man or a boy, whose
high cast arcs forever
through the peeling sky.

Blind Date

It's this friend sets them up
so they meet one sunny mid-Thursday
at Starbucks, a little wary, yes, but they talk
about his ex, and her son, and their jobs.
She says she'd believed the world
would be fair, and he
sees this in the way she wears her beret,
its little umbilicus like a tiny, hopeful explorer.
She likes that he tips forward to listen
recrossing his legs, and that
to straighten his mind
he clears his throat, a soft sound
but full of intention, and she likes this very much.
On account of her purposeful shoes, he thinks
her kind, in fact, smart and judicious.
And when the end comes, and she says it's late
and he nods that, yes, he agrees, and they're suddenly
awkward, a little cat walks in, a calico cat and sits at her feet,
clearly a sign, she thinks, clearly one of life's
wordless sermons, for it is upon such
gentle fictions the lonely survive.

There sat down, once, a thing on Henry's heart só heavy

– from Dream Song 29, John Berryman

I knew a Henry.
Henry Almond had the room across the hall on
Buena Vista Street in Cambridge, Central Square.
I was twenty-one and he was twice my age
and then some but we drove from Boston
out to Oregon that tar-melting mid-July
so broke we coasted when we could
and slept inside his day-glo green
Caprice, no rear window, no back seat.

But it was the moment we set out
he said he'd left his wife a year ago,
That bitch, good riddance, and except for baseball and his
preteen problem son that's all he said until just inside
Ohio, touching the brakes.
he said, I let her down.

I didn't ask him what he meant – that ancient,
disappointed soul had barely spoken
in the rooming house – but here beside me
in his wheezy, stinking metal box he felt –
I didn't know – he felt he had to talk,
or ought to talk about his shame, his life, his guilt,
his wife. You know, Jesus Christ, he said but
he was quiet then, or mostly quiet,
all the way through Illinois
and Indiana clear to Cedar Rapids.

I'd driven half the afternoon and all that morning,
and we were resting at a two-pump Spur –
you don't see them now – when, suddenly,
punching the glove box once and then again
and again until the latch broke, Henry said,
She'd drink is what it really was,

and I couldn't mention it, he said, I wouldn't,
she was sweet and generous, mostly, you know
and then she'd get so mean she'd say things,
shout things, You're a queer,
and, You were never anything to me, or
I'm looking for a new place with a real man.
You know, and I'd have argued back, Henry said,

I'd start to, but that's the way it is with alcohol, or, anyway,
with her it was, there'd be this chaos-crazy, screaming
rage and so I'd stand there – why make it worse? –
stand there and stand there until
she'd finished up and gone to bed, and then
I'd drive the ten blocks east to Safeway where I'd walk
along the dairy isle to pet food.

Listen. I was glad to see her go, so
sayonara, adios, except I missed her.
I know I should have, maybe, hung in there,
she loved me and that counts for something, there's
such a thing as loyalty, it's just, I couldn't take the shouting,
you know, I was weaker than I let on, and that was part of it,
so I'd stand there by the kibbles sobbing
like a goddamn lunatic.

Henry cracked his door
and watched a crow wing by.
His voice was softer now, adhesive, spent.
He said, The Sox are strong this year,
we're going places, I can feel it.

Lester and Helen

Maybe that's what God is: It just happens.
– Overheard in a hospital elevator

A man steps out to buy bread and arrives at the store
to find he's left his keys and his wallet
locked away in his room.
Maybe later he'll say, It just happens,
but for now he walks around downtown
and gets lost and spends the day
in a park where a young woman's chasing
her best friend's collie. Since Lester has a way
with animals he and Helen round up the collie
and talk dogs a little.
The leash broke, Helen says.
It's chilly, so Lester offers his coat.
They laugh and have coffee, and Lester
asks can he see her again. They go to the show,
hold hands, marry and have two sons, Bill and Jack.
And this is not magic.
Or no more than how we picture both
boys in knickers and place them in school.
Imagine the 30s.
Black, wide-fendered cars line the streets and the boys
wear caps and Jack carries his books in a green canvas bag.
Bill carries his with a strap.
In a few years Bill's
off to college where someone says,
One day I'll introduce you to Margaret.
Bill's shy – first he will, and then he won't.
And then he will.
So they meet and they order the cold plate, talk,
talk, talk: Bill loves science, Margaret loves books,
and they marry and forty years later they finally divorce.
Still, whatever they say and however events

come together and dates add up, this
is where my own life starts.
The truth is it couldn't have happened otherwise.
And that it just happened.

What It's Like

It's like you look back
and there's the first half of forever
which was nothing to you since you were nothing
yourself but there it is stretching way
beyond the beginning
of the beginning of anything
because it is the first half of everything
which is what the absence of you had been zipping through,
and so imagine your exits – Stone Age, Age of Reason,
Renaissance, etc., or, say, 8902 BC, or 1396, or 1464
or 1982, or maybe when the landscape finally
looks familiar or attractive or instructive enough –
someone – who but you? but there is no you – somebody
says, Well, this looks pretty good,
and so all these tiny bits of carbon and hydrogen,
nitrogen, and calcium, phosphorus, sodium and sulfur
copper, zinc, iron and bromide
clump up in somebody's belly, clump and grow,
clump and grow until you spring forth
in a bathroom south of Akron or a cab in New Delhi,
a bedroom in Ames or a pool hall in Brixton or an ER in Boston
which is what it's like exactly, except, *except*
pretty soon you're wondering why
you couldn't remember to remember
that route a little bit, goddamn it,
your roots because now here you are
and it's the middle of the night and you're in the kitchen
scanning the classified or thumbing a catalogue
or slicing a pie and you look up
and there's the stove clock saying
2:10 and you're all
wound up about nothing again.

Non, je ne regrette rien: Edith Piaf in Concert

– www.youtube.com

So, here's Edith Piaf, widow and orphan,
fists clenched and tipped forward
for emphasis: No, she sings,
I regret nothing, not the good,
not the bad.
And you want to believe it too,
you're trying to believe it, and you
who should have married or moved sing along.
You who could have done more sing along.
You who should have done less,
you with the snazzy bow tie, you
in the aisle seat closest the exit, sing along.
You who should have kept still, you who should
have spoken, you say it too, and you in the blue
shoes, and you in the yellow dress:
No, I regret nothing.
Or think of the eighth-grade world wall-map
with the different colored countries and the great
green sea – behind it, against the blackboard there
had to be some alternate, opposite map,
one showing the world where whatever
went wrong turned out fine in the end.
But you, sir, and you, mister,
think how the heart, atop its substrata
of explication and excuse, wants one more chance,
and you ticking softly away in the sad room
over the feed grain store, and you, and you,
the lady now standing,
the one just starting to clap, and you, mister,
and you, the one now bringing one hand
to your mouth – think of it, say it, sing it,
sing it again.

– for Stephanie Brown

What the Dead Know

They know to keep quiet.
But they would tell you don't worry.
They would tell you there's
sloping gentle fields and a marvelous light.
They'd whisper, Mister,
take it easy, they would signal Madam, buy a hat.
They would tell you start again, rent a room, move
forward, breathe a little, read a little,
take a walk, watch your step.
They would tell you God
wears plaid pants, six-eyelet
Oxfords, and a wrist watch, Helbros, gold.
They would tell you God's
a girl in third grade knotting Her shoe.
They would tell you God's a man with cracked glasses
mowing His yard, or He lives with Lilly,
His wife, and a son named Sal.
They would tell you He works in auto body repair
and plays the guitar.
They would tell you He's thought up Himself,
that He thinks up botany and basketball,
eczema, mustard, and mayhem.
They would tell you He makes up the malls
and the back-alleys, the droplets, and the tiny specks
and spores, and the long, loud parties
that reach deep into the morning and mean
for someone a meeting, for someone
a mating and for someone a crashed
yellow Chevy and a trip to the joint.
They would say, He makes up the frowsy freeways
and the dirty everyday, or that, regarding a white cloud
in the shape of a thumbless glove, He thinks up breakfast
with bacon that sizzles and curls on itself like a lie though He
may never speak of this even to Himself.
What do the dead know?

They've signed on to keep quiet,
but if they could tell you they would,
and if they could they would comfort you.
They'd tell you, Go on and be happy, try it.
You would.

Easy Money

By fifth grade he was pitching pennies,
and by sixth grade he was flipping for dimes, or
we all were, or some of us, but this was mostly
Billy's thing and in no time he'd advanced
to quarters with the older kids.
Wanna bet? he'd say,
and biting his lip and leaning forward,
he would barely breathe.

Once, after Larry Rizzitano cleaned
him out in home room he was in the lunch line
when I watched him stake his coat against
fat Jack Hudson's chocolate milk.
He'd had this edgy, out-there
look like he might
just strike it rich right now or
screw it, lose it all, though when he did,
at last, finally, when he lost it all, it was winter 1968,
a Friday night, and it was in his mother's Galaxy.
The Rizzitano kid had shotgun, Bill Franks
and Bobby Rader rode in back.
They'd been topping ninety someone said,
hit an ice patch, rolled, and slammed a phone pole.

Sometimes, reaching for change, I think of a quarter
moving from a Brink's truck with a bag of other money
to a bank some place in Delaware or Philly.
Pocket to pay phone, change purse to pharmacy,
Key West to Baton Rouge, I think of it moving,
moving down those sixteen years until
one night, flipped skywards,
faintly ringing, rising
like a little moon, it starts to fall.

– for Billy O'Malley (1952 – 1968)

Baffled

It was always in the evening.
It was always after supper when my sister
stood outside my room, and leaning, leaning in
so as not to touch my stuff, she'd whisper
in her most complicit, lowered
tone, Mom's crying.
There was worry with a warning in it
so we'd walk slowly by the kitchen past
my mother sobbing near the sink, arms crossed,
still pretty in her thirties in the Sixties, and she'd turn away.
Behind her somewhere rooted near the fridge
or by the radio, my father, slowly with a certain
emphasis, I don't know what you *want,* he'd say.

So I guess she didn't feel like telling him, or
if she did, she wouldn't because he should have known.
It's not so strange.
But I could be his father now,
and of an early summer, in a back yard just
like this, I could tell him, sad, baffled, silent man,
I could say exactly what was wrong and what to do.
I could. I almost could.

Arthur

Anger doesn't catch the light like laughter,
but with my friend it seems to crowd him,
seems to complicate his neck and jaw.
It's not just that.
It's made him fat.
We've only walked two blocks
and he's wheezing when we reach Walgreens.
A wind-fixed scent of diesel passes.
I hate my job, he says, I'm tired,
and my friends don't call.

Of course, there's always the traffic and the weather
and the war but it used to be the slob next door
and before they split up it was always
the missus: no zip, no spark,
no spunk, too calm by half –
calm when his car died, calmer when
the lawn caught fire,
still calmer in the primal act.
But it's not the job he can't stand
(though it is and he can't) it's the people
and the pay and we pause and later back home
finally closing my eyes there's the usual slow-motion
stars and ambient blues and unblacks and I think
of this friend, so sad, and peevish and pudgy,
collapsing slowly into himself,
an arithmatic of battered will
and bungled choice.
And who's exempt?
Hopeful or angry or afraid, it's
being here, living here, and going along
at the center of a perfect, unattainable present
as if some bruised and tumbling private sky were
moving in, the soft, random patter of rain.

Hat

I'm together with three friends
smoking a bowl and we're talking cars, then books
then bars and Asian fruit and formica tile when
I suddenly think, I don't have a clue.
Still, I sit there.
I look around but I sit there because,
well, what are we *talking* about and because
I know I'm missing something, in fact,
I'm missing the whole point here, not
just tonight but maybe
I've missed the whole point of everything all along:
I don't get it, listen, I thought I might but I don't but
I'm trying to stay calm, I'm trying
to relax *except* nothing's
what it seems and nothing's wholly actual,
and true and real and right, but you
know how it is, you know what
I'm saying: this why you have to love
the hipster's use of "like", not "like"
meaning indicative of as in, Looks
like disaster, and not " like" meaning
inclined to as in He felt like taking off, but "like"
meaning closely resembling, "like" meaning similar to,
"like" as it's strewn through speech like magnesium
in squash because as far as the real and the right
now, here's what we've got: approximate,
nearly, somewhat, and almost, similar
and resembling, and so I take off my hat
to the beats, I do, or it's like I do, it's like
I take off my figurative hat, the hat
with the feather and the phony jewel,
the hat with the chin strap and curved bill,
the hat with the button saying "Peace",
the patch saying "Breathe".

The Cat and the Fiddle

In the scene where the cow jumps
over the moon the little dog laughs
with his mouth wide open.
Comforted by the same thirty words
he's heard fifty times the boy leans sideways
into his mother.
Before this they'd walked by the water.
Before that they'd spread their blanket on
the grassy bank, and before that
the mother looked straight ahead and thought
of how she might change her whole life starting,
starting soon –
and how like an adult.
And how like these two to fish and say poems
at the wrong time completely.
Before the short drive to the lake,
before certain words at the stove,
they'd sat with the dad in the kitchen.
And couldn't the boy just listen, for once?
No. No, he wouldn't know good luck or good news
if they'd spanked him in unison.
You see here is a child who any more to keep
after what good would it do?
Meat loaf night.
The lights of the cabana shine over the water.
The mother and son sip warm Cokes on the pier.
Now the boy leans sideways resting his head.
And how like the fat cat to fiddle
and play like nothing's amiss,
and how like the grinning dish to lift high
its inconsequent legs and speed away
when its place is at home.

Home Movie

July 4, 1965

Saxophone and trombone, trumpet,
trumpet, trumpet. And there's Roxanne
and Dick and Betty Mayfield and the Laurie girls.
But isn't that George Betts on clarinet?
Of course, it's all so grainy though,
which is just as it should be because here
we suddenly actually *were*, or, and *isn't* that
Malcolm Sproul and Claudia Benck?
And wouldn't that be Dick French and there's
that wiseacre, Billy Orvis, and Arthur Fraze.
And now, somehow, look, someone
in somebody's yard, someone,
a boy in a foot-deep plastic pool,
skidding sideways and pitching forwards,
euphoric in jaunty fedora, a giddy private eye
in blue shirt and shorts,
waves once and as his mother laughs
she turns, and with her, wistful and trying
and troubled by longings, there's Mr Yastremian,
and beside him with the drink, Jim Sterling with my best
friend's strange father, Dr. Morensy, and quickly someone
else, and someone and someone
and then, no, *yes*, that's, that's What's-Her-Name,
judicious and afflicted, and nice enough, yes, and yet,
there's some way she tips forward, or inwardly anyway,
necessitous and over-eager, but tuning in as if
picking out the faintest oracular tappings.
There's the Roundies with the Levi boy.
And there's that flirty, sparking Mrs. Archer –
and, sure, and *now,* now I want to run it all again.
Oh friends, where were we going
in that shaky dawn?

The Uncertainty Principle

I'm watching a young woman
step over the curb and into the street
simultaneously slopping her latte into her purse
and jab-jabbing her first finger into her gangly male
friend as she speaks.
We were like *nearly* there, she says.
We were like *almost* there, okay, and you're like,
you're like let's turn around and so we do,
naturally, because it's like you
always get your way.
Meantime the man friend
walks slowly along nodding *Yes,* and *Sure,*
and Abso*lute*ly, but he's mostly thumbing the slick,
flat, folding gizmo in his hand and not
seeing the light so much as taking the heat
which is building to boiling more quickly than ever.
So, I'm sorry, he says, *Okay?*
Still, as my bus arrives she's resumed
this poke-poking away, and I'm trying not
to look, but even as I board, and even as I'm
taking my seat, I'm replaying
the whole scene in my mind's eye because
who can say I'm not a little to blame, like maybe
my cap or bent glasses, jacket, belt and chipped tooth
remind her of drunk Uncle Ed, or her traveling dad,
or her second-to-best boyfriend's
final snarling remark. I mean,
it's like that theory in science:
If you want to test something,
you have to look at it except the looking
changes everything:
It's like there *is* no This is what happened
and there is no This is what *would* have happened
if you hadn't stuck your big schnoz in. In fact, maybe
my yellowish shirt or new shoes point her life to

speed knitting or integral calculus, and by the next block
I'm thinking of what subtle, inexplicable winds
steer my own life, so that later, back home,
at rest on the big green sofa,
I notice the faintest breeze riffling the pages
of my opened bills, and through the curtains
and over the trees there's the tumbling
summer sky and though the evening
seems perfect it's as if I'm already missing it,
and missing the day I've had, the squabbling couple,
the bus, the sofa, and the moon, and the mail, and then
wishing I weren't, and so don't,
so do.

Cinderella at the Twilite Motel

She was pretty, he was rich, she went along.
But she was sick of those slippers from the get-go –
garish and tight, they gave her the jimmy legs.
Then, one night, years later, he's out
on the town, she's watching tv,
when she throws the remote,
packs a dress and a coat,
and finding money and keys
splits, drives around, checks in about six.
She reads a little, makes a drink,
and orders Chinese.
A car's booming bass disappears by the note.
Of course, she ought to feel free but
she's nervous and sad.
It's cold for November.
Freightliners idle in the lot next door,
but there's the phone.
Hello? she says and Hel-*lo,* he says,
like that, like a regular prince, except
she knows the tone, like this is all her fault,
like she's been leading him on, and as
inevitable as the thought she might
have had another, better life, she pictures him
picture her: naked in pumps, nude in her sandals, bare
in her bed with her high heels on.
Don't take this wrong, she says,
I don't want to be mean, she says, but
you give me the creeps, and she hangs up
and steps out. A siren flares, trees sway,
and the sky, there is no sky.
She'll walk by the water.
Over the highway, and after the mall,
the lake so still beyond the shadowing pines,
this is where she thinks about life, this life,
her life, a blessing and a tired weight,

that long-hurdling arc between
whereever she'd started and whatever's
ahead, that strange and constant counting down
without which there'd be nothing to say.

Alan

Once, thirty years ago at six a.m.,
I saw Alan Douglas again.
He was outside Bev's Tap when I passed
and waiting already, already shaky, and when
we'd said hello and walked a ways
Alan asked me had I heard
about his case.

No, I said.
Well, he'd had this big break thanks
to a loophole in the law.
I hadn't heard.
See, it was all about a statue of limitations, Alan said.
which struck me funny, like an obelisk to mishap,
or a monument to failure, say, a soldier
on a rearing charger cast in bronze surrounded
by some spurting fountains and a fancy pool
except the horse would be a collie
and the sword would be a toilet brush.

Then Allen asked me if I'd have just one
and I said, No thanks, so Alan said,
Oh, one little beer because what's
the big deal anyway, and I said
that wasn't the point.
The point?
I guessed if he was thirsty he was lonely too.
But I had no point.

We'd paused by Norman Dry Goods.
Alan turned and headed back to Bev's.
I had on blue jeans plus this kind of sweater-jacket thing.

Traveling Through the Dark

Say you turn off County B
and up Prospect into the soft
swale of early autumn, park
and start walking. You pass a beat Camry
with a crumpled trunk, then a man in a knit cap.

But say it's late.
A little plastic leaps over the curb
with a posse of leaves,
and through the elm straight ahead
the whole sky is moving.
You know what I'm saying.

Up the block someplace someone
shouts, Honey come in please,
shouts, Sweetheart it's dark out.
But you know what I'm talking about:
You wonder how the gentle arc of your life
has landed you here, here on Prospect Street,

but here in Somerville or Milton,
here with a bumped door flying open,
here with your two not quite friends yet friends
stepping into the flickery light and waving Hello,
and, How *are* you, How are you
and, Glad you could be here.

Memorial

It was early spring of course, midweek,
and late afternoon, and everyone you loved was there.
Your children were there, your brother
was there, some work friends
and neighbors, and even the Hendes came.

A few of us set out flowers,
and arranged the chairs, and then,
restive and sad,
we waited around.
We waited in our good shoes
and our dresses and suits.
We waited on the steps outside.

But I want to say how the sun finally shone.
It was just spring, you know, and it had been the worst
winter, and through the leaves the sky bloomed
a dazzling brilliant blue,
and we watched the traffic passing.
We watched some students playing soccer
in the park next door.
Then, once, a plastic bag
cart-wheeled over the sidewalk
and collapsed at the curb, and two robins landed,
looked on and listened, hopped
and flew off.

At the corner we saw
a young woman peering under somebody's car.
She was disheveled and heavy
and began to leave but came back
and began to cry and call out, Here Kitty,
she was saying, on her hands and knees.
Here Kitty.
It was late afternoon.

Two of us walked over to help,
and she said she was grateful.
Thanks, she said, Thank you, she said.
It was just spring, and it was Wednesday
and you were gone.

– for W. L. Kraushaar

A Note About Mark Kraushaar

Mark Kraushaar was born in Washington DC and grew up outside Boston in Concord, Massachusetts. He attended Marlboro College in Vermont, where he studied literature and writing, worked briefly as a high school English teacher, then as a cab driver in Boston. After this, he moved to London for two years and travelled in Europe. Back in the States he lived for a time in New York City and again in Boston. He attended trade school in Louisville, Kentucky, worked as a welder on the coal and grain barges on the Mississippi and then moved to the state of Mississippi, where he worked as a pipe welder at Ingalls Shipbuilding. He moved to Wisconsin after two years at the shipyard, worked in construction as a pipe welder but found this was "definitively not my dish" and so went to nursing school in Madison, Wisconsin. He has worked as an RN in Madison since the mid-80s. His work has appeared in the *Hudson Review*, *Ploughshares*, *Alaska Review*, *Gettysburg Review*, as well as *Best American Poetry*, and the website *Poetry Daily*. He has been featured in the *Missouri Review* as well as *Michigan Quarterly* and has been a recipient of *Poetry Northwest*'s Richard Hugo Award. A previous collection, *Falling Brick Kills Local Man*, was a finalist for the May Swenson Award, the Juniper Prize and the Walt Whitman Award, and was published in 2009 by the University of Wisconsin Press as winner of the Felix Pollak Prize.

A Note About the Anthony Hecht Poetry Prize

The Anthony Hecht Poetry Prize was inaugurated in 2005 and is awarded on an annual basis to the best first or second collection of poems submitted.

2005
Judge: J. D. McClatchy
Winner: Morrie Creech, *Field Knowledge*

2006
Judge: Mary Jo Salter
Winner: Erica Dawson, *Big-Eyed Afraid*

2007
Judge: Richard Wilbur
Winner: Rose Kelleher, *Bundle o' Tinder*

2008
Judge: Alan Shapiro
Winner: Carrie Jerrell, *After the Revival*

2009
Judge: Rosanna Warren
Winner: Matthew Ladd, *The Book of Emblems*

2010
Judge: James Fenton
Winner: Mark Kraushaar, *The Uncertainty Principle*

For further information, please send an SASE to the press or visit its website:

http://waywiser-press.com/hechtprize.html